GRAPHIC MODERN HISTORY
WORLD WAR I

GALLIPOLI
AND THE SOUTHERN THEATERS

By Gary Jeffrey & Illustrated by Terry Riley

 Crabtree Publishing Company
www.crabtreebooks.com

Crabtree Publishing Company

www.crabtreebooks.com

Created and produced by:
David West Children's Books

Project development, design, and concept:
David West Children's Books

Author and designer: Gary Jeffrey

Illustrator: Terry Riley

Editor: Lynn Peppas

Proofreader: Crystal Sikkens

Project coordinator: Kathy Middleton

Print and production coordinator:
Katherine Berti

Prepress technician: Katherine Berti

Photographs: p5t, NASA

Library and Archives Canada Cataloguing in Publication

Jeffrey, Gary
    Gallipoli and the southern theaters / Gary Jeffrey ;
illustrated by Terry Riley.

(Graphic modern history : World War I)
Includes index.
Issued also in electronic formats.
ISBN 978-0-7787-0911-4 (bound).
--ISBN 978-0-7787-0917-6 (pbk.)

    1. World War, 1914-1918--Campaigns--Balkan Peninsula--
Juvenile literature. 2. World War, 1914-1918--Campaigns--
Turkey--Gallipoli Peninsula--Juvenile literature. 3. World War,
1914-1918--Campaigns--Balkan Peninsula--Comic books, strips,
etc. 4. World War, 1914-1918--Campaigns--
Turkey--Gallipoli Peninsula--Comic books, strips, etc. 5.
Graphic novels. I. Riley, Terry II. Title. III. Series: Jeffrey, Gary.
Graphic modern history. World War I.

D560.J35 2013   j940.4'147   C2013-901127-7

Library of Congress Cataloging-in-Publication Data

Jeffrey, Gary.
 Gallipoli and the southern theaters / Gary Jeffrey & illustrated
by Terry Riley.
   pages cm. -- (Graphic modern history: World War I)
 Includes index.
 ISBN 978-0-7787-0911-4 (reinforced library binding) -- ISBN
978-0-7787-0917-6 (pbk.) -- ISBN 978-1-4271-9254-7 (electronic
pdf) -- ISBN 978-1-4271-9178-6 (electronic html)1. World War,
1914-1918--Campaigns--Turkey--Gallipoli Peninsula--Comic
books, strips, etc. 2. World War, 1914-1918--Campaigns--Turkey-
-Gallipoli Peninsula--Juvenile literature. 3. World War, 1914-
1918--Campaigns--Serbia--Comic books, strips, etc. 4. World
War, 1914-1918--Campaigns--Serbia--Juvenile literature. 5.
Caporetto, Battle of, Kobarid, Slovenia, 1917--Comic books,
strips, etc. 6. Caporetto, Battle of, Kobarid, Slovenia, 1917--
Juvenile literature. 7. Graphic novels. I. Riley, Terry, illustrator.
II. Title.

D568.3.J44 2013
940.4'2--dc23
                              2013005534

Crabtree Publishing Company

www.crabtreebooks.com   1-800-387-7650

Printed in the U.S.A./042013/SX20130306

Published in Canada
Crabtree Publishing
616 Welland Ave.
St. Catharines, Ontario
L2M 5V6

Published in the United States
Crabtree Publishing
PMB 59051
350 Fifth Avenue, 59th Floor
New York, New York 10118

Published in the United Kingdom
Crabtree Publishing
Maritime House
Basin Road North, Hove
BN41 1WR

Published in Australia
Crabtree Publishing
3 Charles Street
Coburg North
VIC 3058

CONTENTS

OPENING BATTLES

Serbia (beige) sat at the base of the Austro-Hungarian Empire (orange)— from a 1905 map.

Tension between Serbia and her enormous neighbor, Austria-Hungary, provided the spark that ignited World War I in 1914. Serbia had sponsored the assassin who killed the Austrian Archduke Franz Ferdinand, in Sarajevo

A RUSH TO ARMS

Serbia wanted the mainly-Slavic southern part of Austria-Hungary, called Bosnia, to break away and form a greater Serbia. On July 28, 1914, Austria-Hungary declared war on Serbia, and invaded on August 12. Determined to win a battle before the emperor's birthday on August 18, Austrian commander, Potiorek, attacked at the Battle of Cer with only two small armies that equaled 200,000 men. They faced 180,000 less-trained Serbian soldiers.

AUSTRIA REPULSED

Many of the Austrian soldiers were Slavs and were reluctant to fight fellow Slavs. The Austrian army was forced back past their starting point. Potiorek tried again at the Battle

The Austrian commander, Oskar Potiorek, was keen for vengeance against Serbia.

of Kolubara. This time forcing the Serbian army to abandon Belgrade, Serbia's capital c A brilliant counterattack, coordinated amo three armies by General Zivojin Misic finally ejected the Austrians from Serbia. But the price was high with 170,000 Serb casualties and 215,00 Austro-Hungarian casualties.

The Serbian commander, Radomir Putnik (above), was old and ill, but had a great general in Zivojin Misic (right).

EXPEDITION TO THE DARDANELLES

The Turkish Ottoman Empire joined the Central Powers against the Allies in October 1914. Russia, Britain, and France were part of the Allies. The best sea route for supplying weapons to Russia was now blocked. Britain's First Lord of the Admiralty, Winston Churchill, pushed for an attack in the Dardanelles in the hopes of capturing

The Dardanelles is a narrow strait in northwestern Turkey.

Winston Churchill

the Turkish capital of Constantinople (Istanbul) on the Gallipoli Peninsula. This was the main source of supplies for the Ottoman Empire. The Commander of the British Army, Lord Kitchener, refused to send troops from the deadlocked Western Front, so Churchill organized a mainly naval expedition, reinforced with Australian Imperial Forces and New Zealand troops (together known as ANZACS).

British navy

FIRST STRIKES

In March 1915, an Anglo-French fleet tried to force its way up the straits ahead of the main force. Helped by the Germans, the Turks had secretly laid a minefield where the Allied ships were gathered, destroying three battleships and damaging many more.

British battleship HMS Irresistible lies sinking, on March 18, 1915— a victim of Turkish mines.

The Dardanelles could not be opened by ship alone. Ground troops were made ready for landing. Meanwhile, Italy had been persuaded to declare war on Austria-Hungary on May 24, 1915.

The Allied Italian Commander, Luigi Cadorna, had steadily built up his armies.

TWO DEADLOCKS AND A ROUT

Mediterranean Expeditionary Force commander, Sir Ian Hamilton, planned a three-point assault at Gallipoli. Navy troops would land on the tip, and French troops on the opposite tip (in a feint). The main attackers would be the **ANZACS,** halfway up on the western side.

Boats loaded with ANZACS arrive to secure the beach on the Gallipoli Peninsula on April 25, 1915.

SLUGGING MATCH

The ANZACS landed, at first light, a mile (1.6 km) north of their intended position. Their route was now blocked by rugged cliffs. After rushing the slopes and taking a ridge, they were driven back to the cliff edge by a powerful Turkish counterattack. As they held on, their commander, Birdwood, asked for evacuation. Hamilton requested he stand firm, and ordered his men to "dig, dig, dig."

Meanwhile, on the tip at Helles, a massacre was underway as British regiments came under intense fire. By nightfall, they had landed, but were too broken to advance. Gallipoli settled into a trench warfare stalemate, lifted only when the whole force was evacuated in late 1915—a mishandled and tragic Allied failure.

Along with ANZAC troops, were soldiers like the Royal Naval Division, seen here rushing into attack. In the end, both sides lost over 200,000 men.

Uphill Struggle

Italy had joined the war to gain Austrian land, in the northwest of its border, that contained Italian-speaking people. In mid-1915, Cadorna had 35 divisions facing 20 Austrian divisions. Warfare took place in the mountainous region along the Isonzo River. The Austrians faced supply problems over the mountains, but held the high ground. This gave them an advantage.

The Italian front was shaped like an "s" on its side. The main battlegrounds were on the Isonzo River on the right-hand edge.

   Cadorna believed in moving frontal attacks in the hopes of pushing back the Austrians. When wave after wave of his soldiers were disastrously defeated against the strong Austrian defenses, he simply dug in his heels, and demanded that the uphill frontal assaults continue.

Italian troops on the line of the Isonzo

The first four battles alone cost 161,000 Italian casualties and 147,000 Austrian. There would be seven more before the Battle of Caporetto. Italian discipline was harsh. Cadorna even re-introduced Roman decimation, which is the killing of every tenth soldier in a unit if the unit failed to perform in battle.

The Agony of Serbia

Failure at Gallipoli, and a successful German offensive against Russia, convinced neutral Bulgaria to join the Central Powers on October 1, 1915. Serbia was attacked from the east by Bulgaria and from the north by Germany. Her weakened army was no match for either.

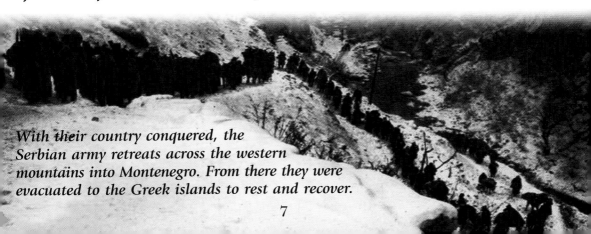

With their country conquered, the Serbian army retreats across the western mountains into Montenegro. From there they were evacuated to the Greek islands to rest and recover.

IN THE FIRST BATTLE FOR SERBIA

NEAR SHABATZ, IN WESTERN SERBIA, NOVEMBER 15, 1914

ERNST ENZMANN, A PRIVATE IN THE AUSTRIAN FIFTH ARMY, WATCHED AS THE CAPTAIN THEY CALLED "THE LOUSE" BEAT A SOLDIER WHO HAD FALLEN DURING THE MARCH...

GET UP! GET UP, YOU LAZY GOOD-FOR-NOTHING!

DOESN'T HE UNDERSTAND HOW HUNGRY AND EXHAUSTED WE **ALL** ARE?

THEIR MARCH, SINCE INVADING ACROSS THE BOSNIAN BORDER, HAD TAKEN THEM FAR AHEAD OF THE REGIMENT'S FIELD KITCHEN.

LATER, ENZMANN WAS STANDING GUARD WHEN...

OH, MY STOMACH...

GROINNNNNK!

THE LOUSE'S ORDERLY— WHAT'S HE GOT THERE?

SAUSAGES?!

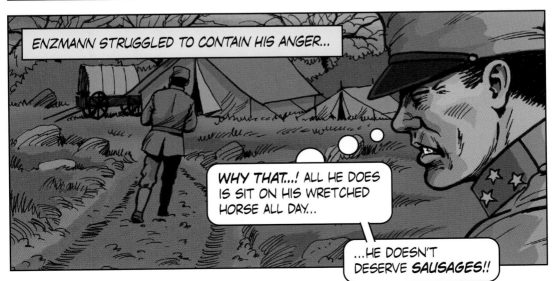

ENZMANN STRUGGLED TO CONTAIN HIS ANGER...

WHY THAT...! ALL HE DOES IS SIT ON HIS WRETCHED HORSE ALL DAY...

...HE DOESN'T DESERVE *SAUSAGES!!*

THE NEXT DAY, AS THEY ADVANCED TO THE FRONT...

GRAY CLOUDS EXPLODING OVERHEAD—UH, OH...

IT WAS A BOMBARDMENT OF HEAVY ARTILLERY.

THEIR FIRST...

KROOM!

HIGH EXPLOSIVE SHELLS RAINED THICK AND FAST, BREAKING THEIR LINES.

BA-BOOM!

ENZMANN SEARCHED DESPERATELY FOR SHELTER.

HE WATCHED AS A SHELL SCREAMED OVERHEAD, KNOCKING THE HAT OFF A SOLDIER.

PHWEEEEAAAR

IN A DAZE, THE MAN DUSTED OFF HIS HAT AS THE DUD PLOWED UP EARTH BEHIND HIM.

PLUMPF!

ENZMANN FOUND SHELTER BEHIND A HOUSE FOR A MOMENT, BEFORE SPRINTING FORWARD.

HE REACHED A SUNKEN ROAD AS THE HOUSE WAS BLOWN TO FRAGMENTS.

BER-DOOM!

AS THE SERBS FELL BACK, THE AUSTRIANS ADVANCED AFTER THEM INTO THE HILLS.

WHY DO THEY MAKE US CROSS OPEN GROUND IN THE DAYLIGHT?

IT'S STUPID, BUT I GUESS OUR LIVES ARE CHEAP TO THEM...

THEY REACHED GROUND THAT HAD BEEN RECENTLY FOUGHT OVER.

LOOK AT THESE MEN!

THEIR UNIFORMS LOOK NEW. THEY MUST BE RECRUITS, FRESH FROM HOME.

ENZMANN MOVED FROM CORPSE TO CORPSE UNTIL...

YOU. YOU LOOK ABOUT MY SIZE...

ENZMANN RELIEVED THE DEAD BOY OF HIS RIFLE, COAT, MONKEY*, SHIRT, AND SHOES.

BUT I'LL LEAVE YOU WITH YOUR PANTS, AND SOME DIGNITY.

HE ALSO FOUND FOOD...

UGH! THE BREAD AND HARDTACK** ARE SOAKED WITH BLOOD.

BUT THESE ARE GOOD.

THEY WERE "IRON RATIONS"— EACH SOLDIER'S EMERGENCY STORE OF FOOD.

NOT TO BE TOUCHED UNLESS ORDERED.

*BACKPACK
**CRACKER OR FLAT BREAD

ON THE EVE OF BATTLE, TWO DAYS LATER, ENZMANN DEFIED REGULATIONS AND BROKE INTO HIS OWN IRON RATIONS...

IN A FEW HOURS, I MAY BE DEAD. IF I SURVIVE, I CAN ALWAYS ROB ANOTHER DEAD MAN.

THEY WERE ORDERED INTO LINES, READY TO ASSAULT LAZAREVAC-A SMALL TOWN NEAR BELGRADE...

...WHEN ARTILLERY RANGED IN ONCE AGAIN.

BLAST!

MORE WASTE AND MADNESS. WHY FORM PARADE LINES THAT WILL DISAPPEAR AS SOON AS WE ATTACK?

NEATLY SILHOUETTED AGAINST THE BURNING HOUSES, THE AUSTRIANS ADVANCED.

AHEAD LAY A FIELD WITH HAYSTACKS. BEYOND THAT WAS A MEADOW OVERLOOKED BY A CHURCH SPIRE...

...FROM WHERE A SERBIAN MACHINE GUN BLAZED.

BLAT-BLAT-BLAT

COME ON, BOYS! FORWARD!

MEN WERE CUT DOWN LEFT AND RIGHT OF HIM AS ENZMANN FLOPPED INTO THE FLOODED MEADOW.

SPLOOSH!

WITH EFFORT, HE FOLLOWED THE LIEUTENANT OVER A LEDGE AND INTO THE TREES.

DRRRRR!

IF YOU CAN DO IT, I CAN DO IT.

HE WENT A FEW PACES, WHEN SUDDENLY THERE WAS A SEARING PAIN IN HIS LEG...

FNNNGH!!

HE WAS FELLED AS IF BY AN AX.

HE BROUGHT HIS HAND UP FROM HIS LEG.

BLOOD?

KRAK!

I'M WOUNDED. THANK GOODNESS—NOW I CAN LEAVE THE BATTLEFIELD.

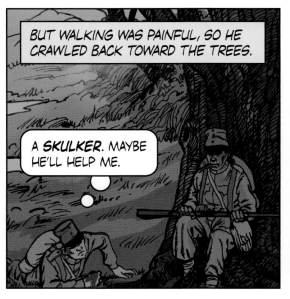

BUT WALKING WAS PAINFUL, SO HE CRAWLED BACK TOWARD THE TREES.

A **SKULKER**. MAYBE HE'LL HELP ME.

THE YOUNG SOLDIER WAS ONLY TOO HAPPY TO LEAVE THE FIELD.

YOU HAVE A FINE SHOT— A GOOD WOUND, JUST A LITTLE HOLE IN THE LEG.

THEY PASSED BY WOUNDED MEN, SOME SERIOUSLY HURT, WHO WERE SHELTERING BEHIND HAYSTACKS.

AAAAAAAAGH—MY LEG!

ENZMANN RECOGNIZED "THE LOUSE."

CAPTAIN, SIR, ARE YOU ALRIGHT?

THE CAPTAIN DIDN'T ANSWER.

HE'S NOT WOUNDED—JUST COWERING IN FRIGHT!

YOU COWARDLY SWINE! YOU SHOULD BE ASHAMED OF YOURSELF!

AT THE DRESSING STATION...

IT WAS A MACHINE GUN BULLET THAT PASSED RIGHT THROUGH.

YOU'RE LUCKY. LUCKIER THAN HIM...

ENZMANN LOOKED OVER AT THE SOLDIER WHO HAD BEEN SHOT IN THE LEG, LIKE HIM, EXCEPT THAT WHERE THE BULLET HAD SPLINTERED IT, SLIVERS OF BONE POKED THROUGH HIS SKIN.

IT WAS PROBABLY A FATAL WOUND.

ENZMANN FELT HIS LUCK THEN. HOPEFULLY, HE WOULD SURVIVE.

THE END

HEROISM AT LONE PINE, GALLIPOLI

THEY STORMED INSIDE. USING BODIES AS SHIELDS, THEY KILLED ANY TURKS REMAINING. IN 20 MINUTES, THE MAIN TRENCH NETWORK HAD BEEN TAKEN.

AAAGH!

YAAAAGH

BANG!

CRACK!

IT HAD BEEN UNEXPECTED, BUT REINFORCEMENTS WERE SENT TO HOLD WHAT THE ANZACS HAD GAINED.

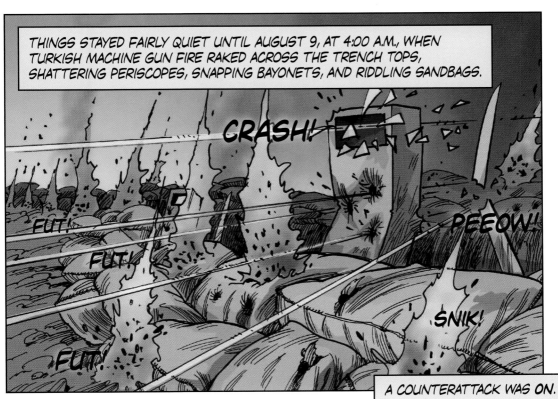

THINGS STAYED FAIRLY QUIET UNTIL AUGUST 9, AT 4:00 A.M., WHEN TURKISH MACHINE GUN FIRE RAKED ACROSS THE TRENCH TOPS, SHATTERING PERISCOPES, SNAPPING BAYONETS, AND RIDDLING SANDBAGS.

CRASH!

FUT!

FUT!

FUT!

PEEOW!

SNIK!

A COUNTERATTACK WAS ON.

LIEUTENANT WILLIAM SYMONS LIT THE FIVE-SECOND FUSE ON A LOTBINIERE BOMB...

GET READY...

RASP

...AND THREW IT TOWARD THE MASS OF ADVANCING TURKS IN GOLDENSTEDT TRENCH.

...HEADS DOWN!

BLOCKED BY A BARRICADE, GOLDENSTEDT LED DIRECTLY INTO ENEMY TERRITORY.

PLOOM!

THEN...

FRED! I'VE GOT TO GO, THE COLONEL NEEDS ME. YOU TAKE OVER, *ALRIGHT?*

OKAY!

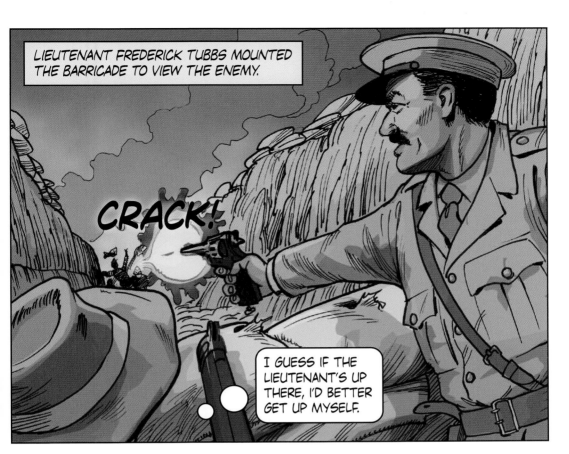

LIEUTENANT FREDERICK TUBBS MOUNTED THE BARRICADE TO VIEW THE ENEMY.

CRACK!

I GUESS IF THE LIEUTENANT'S UP THERE, I'D BETTER GET UP MYSELF.

BANG!

UUUURRRGH...

GOOD BOY!

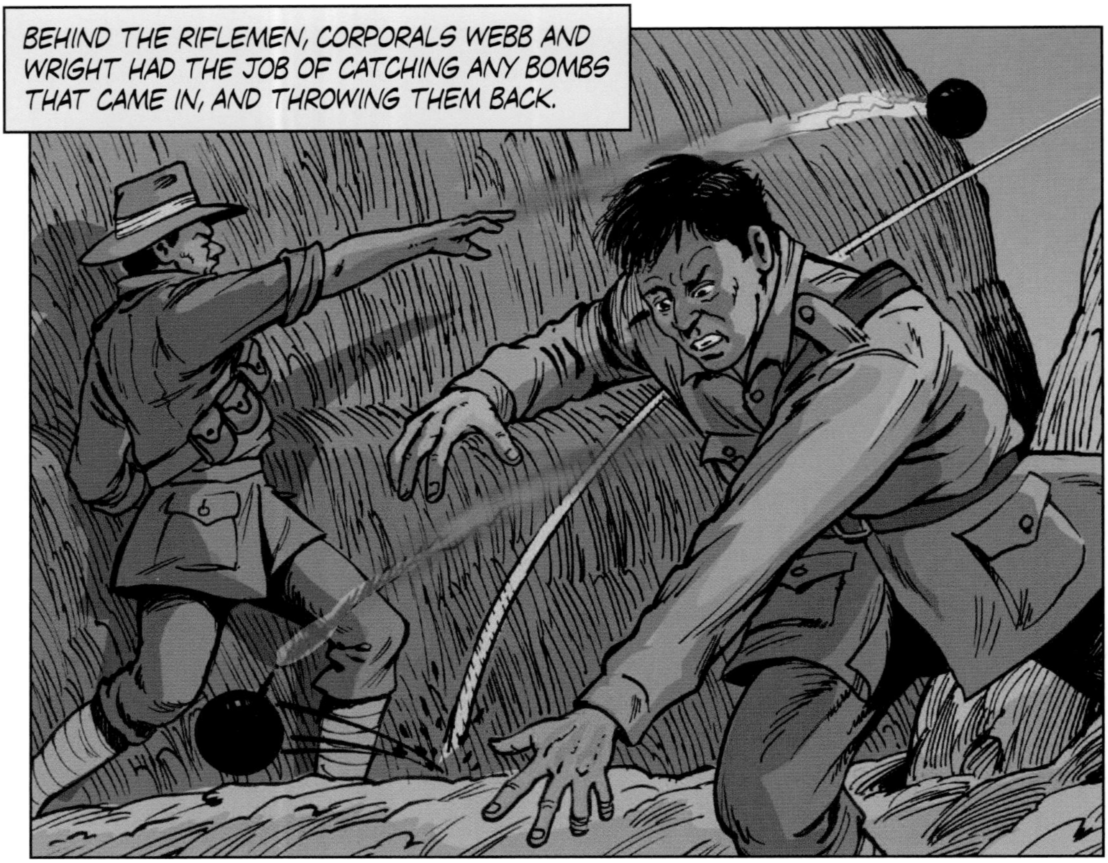
BEHIND THE RIFLEMEN, CORPORALS WEBB AND WRIGHT HAD THE JOB OF CATCHING ANY BOMBS THAT CAME IN, AND THROWING THEM BACK.

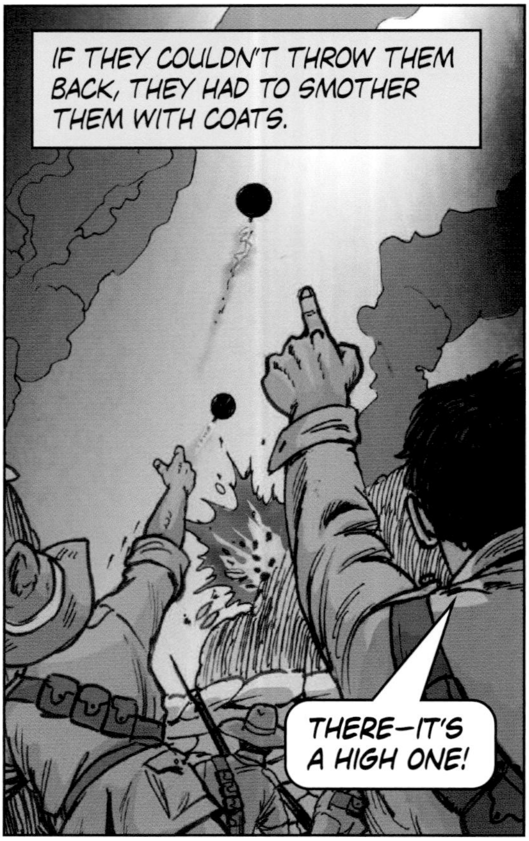
IF THEY COULDN'T THROW THEM BACK, THEY HAD TO SMOTHER THEM WITH COATS.
THERE—IT'S A HIGH ONE!

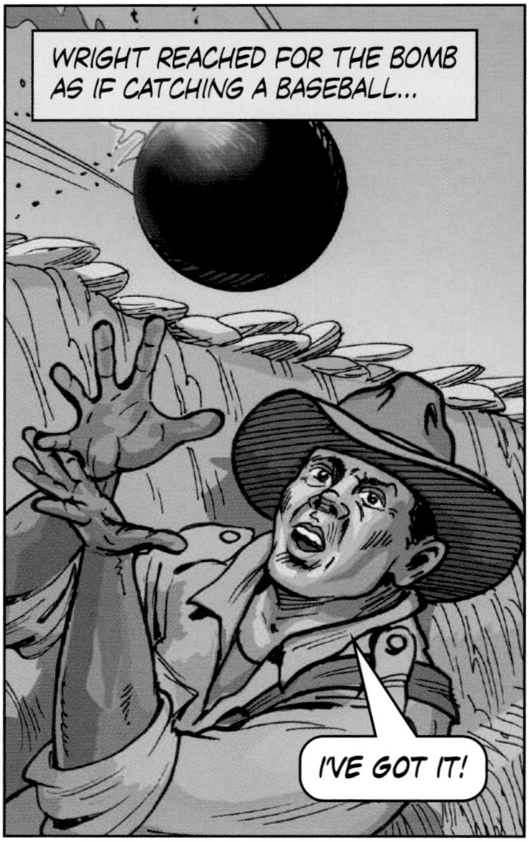
WRIGHT REACHED FOR THE BOMB AS IF CATCHING A BASEBALL...
I'VE GOT IT!

BOOM!

WEBB BARELY HAD TIME TO LOOK BEFORE ANOTHER BOMB SAILED IN.

YOU—

AAAAGH!

BOOM!

TURKS WERE ATTACKING THE TRENCH IN FORCE.

TURKISH BODIES WERE PILING UP BEFORE THE BARRICADE. THEY WERE GOING TO HAVE TO USE BOMBS TO BREAK THROUGH.

CLICK!

ALLAH!

THE BOMBS WERE COMING THICK AND FAST—IT SEEMED IMPOSSIBLE TO CATCH THEM ALL.

ARRRRRGH!

CRACK!

WEBB STAGGERED AWAY. HE HAD LOST BOTH HIS HANDS.

BANG!

BANG!

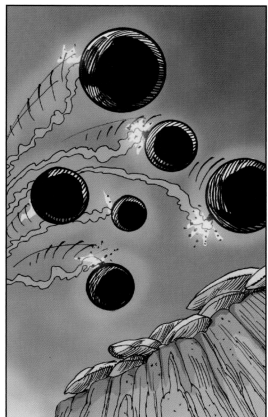

THE GROUP OF BOMBS EXPLODED AMONG TUBBS AND HIS MEN, KILLING FOUR INSTANTLY, AND A FIFTH MINUTES LATER.

BANG!

BANG!

BANG!

BANG!

ONLY TUBBS, WOUNDED IN THE NECK AND ARM, AND CORPORALS DUNSTAN AND BURTON, WERE LEFT TO MAN THE BARRICADE.

CRACK!

KLIK-CLACK!

BLAM!

SUDDENLY, THEIR SANDBAGS WERE BLOWN VIOLENTLY APART.

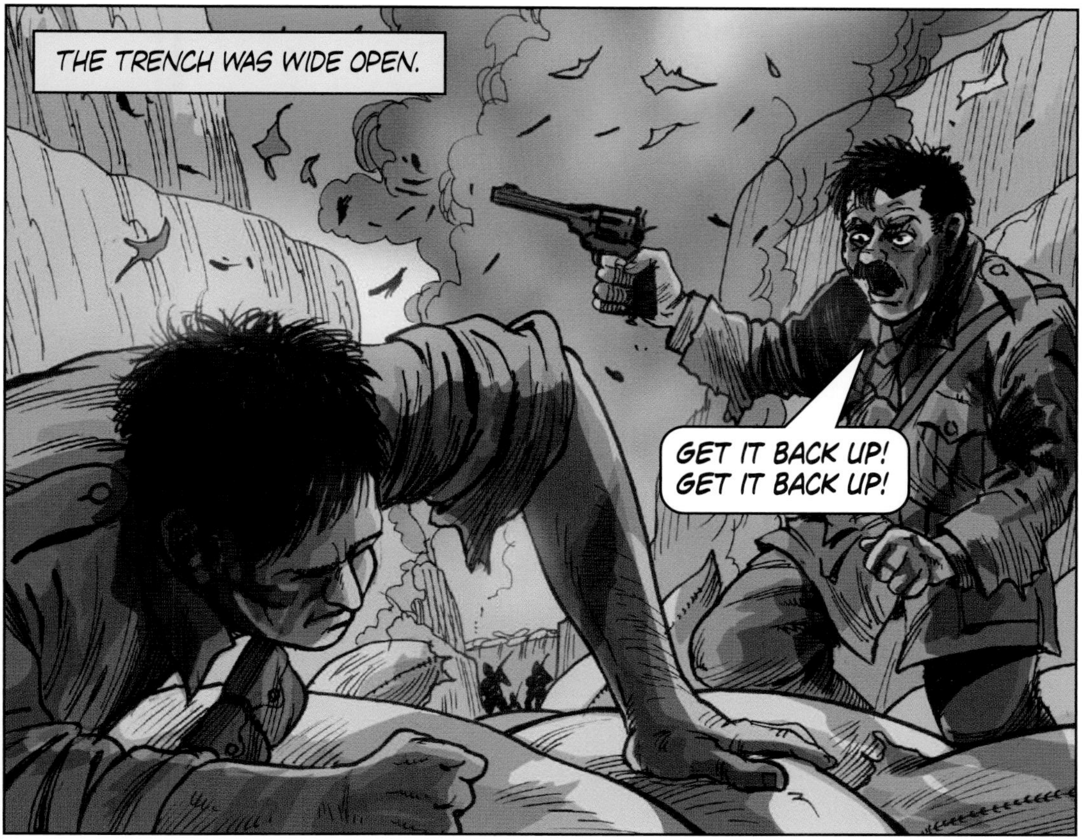
THE TRENCH WAS WIDE OPEN.
GET IT BACK UP! GET IT BACK UP!

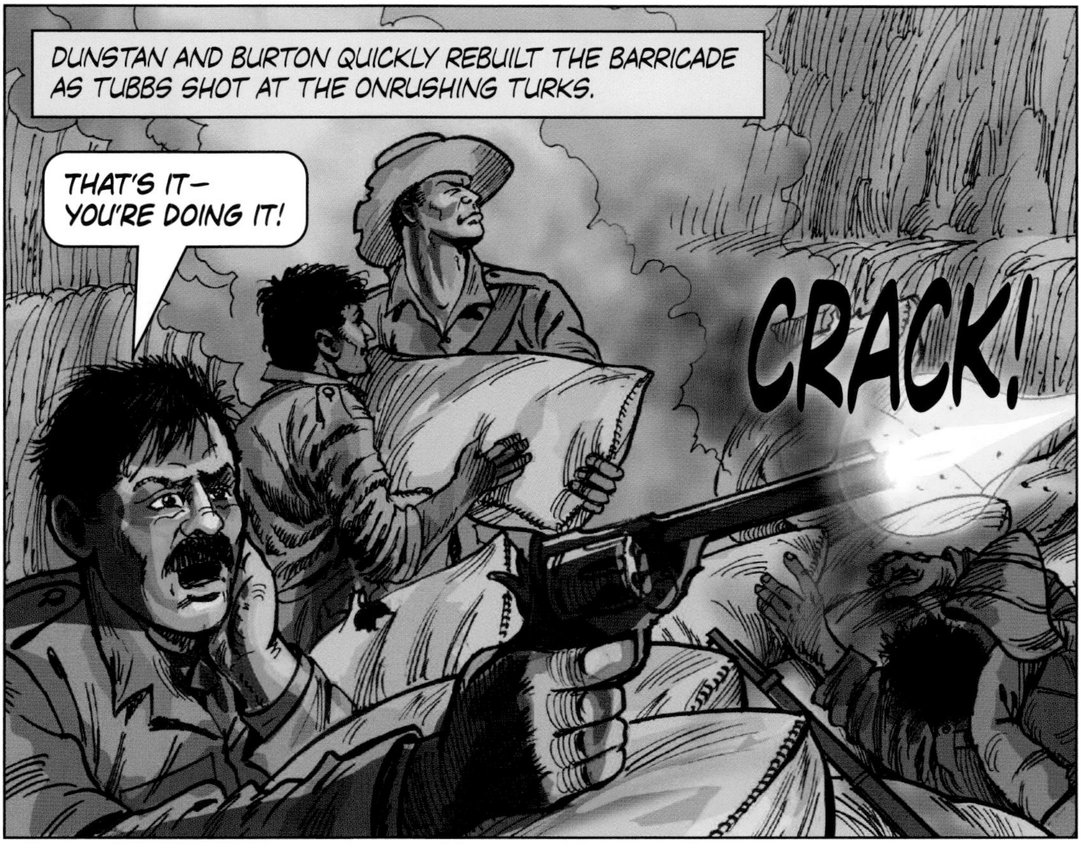
DUNSTAN AND BURTON QUICKLY REBUILT THE BARRICADE AS TUBBS SHOT AT THE ONRUSHING TURKS.
THAT'S IT— YOU'RE DOING IT!
CRACK!

A GRENADE SUDDENLY LANDED BETWEEN DUNSTAN AND BURTON.

OH, NO...

BURTON QUICKLY GRABBED FOR IT.

I'VE—

IT EXPLODED IN A BLINDING FLASH BEFORE HE COULD THROW IT.

FOOM!

DEATH WAS INSTANT.

TUBBS STAGGERED BACK AND SHOUTED FOR HELP.

THEY'RE BREAKING THROUGH!

GNNNGH—I CAN'T SEE...

MEN CAME RUNNING FROM OTHER TRENCHES. THE TURKS WERE DRIVEN BACK.

BANG!

COME ON!

THERE WERE SIMILAR PITCHED BATTLES ALL AROUND LONE PINE, BUT THE AUSTRALIANS HELD ON UNTIL THE AREA WAS ABANDONED, IN THE ALLIED EVACUATION FROM GALLIPOLI IN DECEMBER 1915.

Major Frederick Harold Tubb VC, 1881—1917

Corporal Alexander Stewart Burton VC, 1893—1915

Lieutenant William Dunstan VC, 1895—1957

TUBBS, BURTON, AND DUNSTAN (WHO WAS TEMPORARILY BLINDED) ALL RECEIVED VICTORIA CROSSES FOR THIS ACTION, ALONG WITH FOUR OTHERS, AT THE BATTLE OF LONE PINE.

The Anzac Memorial at Gallipoli, Turkey

THE END

31

THE ROUT AT CAPORETTO

AT 2:00 A.M., ON OCTOBER 24, 1917, LIEUTENANT ERWIN ROMMEL OF THE GERMAN WURTTEMBERG MOUNTAIN REGIMENT WAS WOKEN BY THE THUNDER OF ARTILLERY.

HURRRRRRR...

THE AUSTRIAN GUNS WERE DIRECTED AT THE ITALIAN SECOND ARMY, HOLDING THE UPPER ISONZO BELOW THEM.

ZERO HOUR* FOR THE TROOPS WOULD BE 7:30 A.M.

*START TIME

32

THE WURTTEMBERGERS WERE PART OF A 17-DIVISION STRONG ATTACK FORCE. THEIR MISSION: TO SECURE THE RIDGES AND VALLEYS LEADING TO THE PLAINS OF FRIULI IN ITALY, AND THE ADRIATIC SEA BEYOND.

TOLMEIN

Matajur Mountain

CAPORETTO

Saga

ISONZO RIVER

Flitsch

BY 3:00 A.M., THE ITALIAN HEAVY ARTILLERY AT SAGA LAY BROKEN.

NEXT, THE FIRST OF MORE THAN 2,000 GAS SHELLS WERE LOADED.

THE SHELLS BROKE ONTO INFANTRY POSITIONS GUARDING THE LINE BETWEEN FLITSCH AND SAGA.

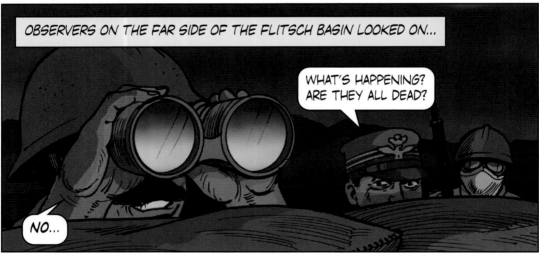

OBSERVERS ON THE FAR SIDE OF THE FLITSCH BASIN LOOKED ON...

WHAT'S HAPPENING? ARE THEY ALL DEAD?

NO...

...THE MEN ARE STILL AT THEIR POSTS. *THE ATTACK HAS FAILED.*

IN FACT, THEY WERE DEAD. THE GAS MASKS HAD FAILED.

THE GAS WAS A NEW WEAPON THAT HAD NOT BEEN USED ON THE ITALIAN FRONT BEFORE.

IN UDINE, AT 5:00 A.M., THE ITALIAN SUPREME COMMANDER, LUIGI CADORNA, ROSE FROM HIS BED.

AS USUAL, HE HAD MILK AND BUTTERED BISCUITS FOR BREAKFAST, AND WROTE TO HIS FAMILY...

"THE MIST AND RAIN FAVORS US, THE DEFENDERS. I FEEL PERFECTLY CALM AND CONFIDENT OF OUR SITUATION..."

AT 6:00 A.M., THERE WAS THE DAILY BRIEFING.

SUPREME COMMANDER, OUR SECOND LINE IS BEING BADLY SHELLED.

BUT NO INFANTRY ASSAULT! IT IS UNDOUBTEDLY A FEINT FOR A BIG ATTACK ON THE CARSO.*

*FAR TO THE EAST

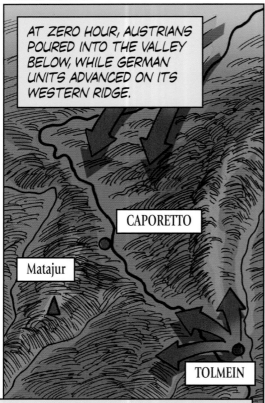

AT ZERO HOUR, AUSTRIANS POURED INTO THE VALLEY BELOW, WHILE GERMAN UNITS ADVANCED ON ITS WESTERN RIDGE.

CAPORETTO

Matajur

TOLMEIN

MEANWHILE, GERMAN AND AUSTRIAN DIVISIONS FANNED OUT FROM TOLMEIN TO CAPTURE THE EASTERN RIDGE.

ROMMEL'S COMPANY COVERED BAVARIAN LIFEGUARDS*, WHO WERE ATTACKING KOLOVRAT RIDGE TO THE WEST.

*ELITE SOLDIERS USED TO PROTECT BAVARIAN KINGS

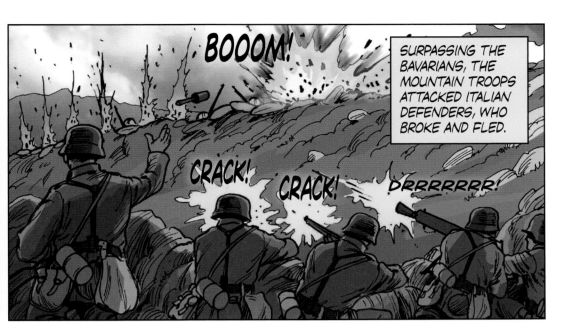

BOOOM!

SURPASSING THE BAVARIANS, THE MOUNTAIN TROOPS ATTACKED ITALIAN DEFENDERS, WHO BROKE AND FLED.

CRACK!

CRACK!

DRRRRRRR!

FEASTING ON CAPTURED RATIONS, ROMMEL AND HIS MEN EYED THE ENEMY-HELD HIGH POINTS THAT LAY AHEAD.

AT 12:15 P.M., CADORNA STILL HAD NO CLUE ABOUT WHAT WAS UNFOLDING.

SO, EXACTLY HOW MANY GUNS CAN THE SECOND ARMY SEND TO THE CARSO?

BY 13:55 P.M., THE CENTRAL POWERS WERE OUTSIDE CAPORETTO, WHILE HUNDREDS OF ITALIAN SOLDIERS STREAMED OUT OF THE TOWN, AWAY FROM THE ISONZO.

OFFICERS PULLED OUT THOSE WITH RIFLES, AND SENT THEM BACK.

SEEING THIS, THE SOLDIERS BEHIND BEGAN TO THROW AWAY THEIR RIFLES.

THEY WERE NOT PREPARED TO DIE TODAY.

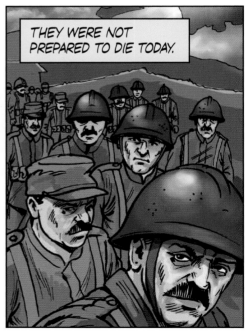

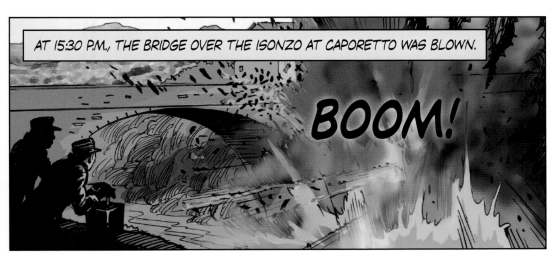

AT 15:30 P.M., THE BRIDGE OVER THE ISONZO AT CAPORETTO WAS BLOWN.

BOOM!

AT THE ITALIAN HEADQUARTERS, REALIZATION WAS DAWNING...

SIR, I'VE LOST CONTACT WITH ANOTHER DIVISION!

SEND IN THE RESERVES!

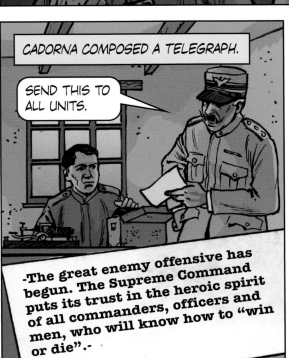

CADORNA COMPOSED A TELEGRAPH.

SEND THIS TO ALL UNITS.

-The great enemy offensive has begun. The Supreme Command puts its trust in the heroic spirit of all commanders, officers and men, who will know how to "win or die".-

THE RESERVES HAD TO PUSH THEIR WAY PAST COLUMNS OF FLEEING MEN.

TURN BACK! THAT WAY IS **DEATH**!

39

BY 12:00 A.M., ON OCTOBER 26, CADORNA AND HIS STAFF HAD EVACUATED UDINE, AND WERE MAKING THEIR WAY PAST FLEEING TROOPS, WHO WERE REJOICING.

NAPOLEON HIMSELF COULD NOT DO ANYTHING IN THESE CONDITIONS!

WHY DOES NO ONE SHOOT THESE MEN?

ROMMEL'S TEAM HAD TAKEN HILL AFTER HILL ON THE RIDGE. HE SIGNALED TO A BATTERY ON THE OTHER SIDE OF THE ISONZO, BY HELIOGRAPH...

CLICK-CLICK-CLICK-CLICK

"TARGET POSITIONS ON HILL 1356."

SHELLS EXPLODED ON THE HILLSIDE, WITH PINPOINT ACCURACY.

MEANWHILE, THE MOUNTAIN TROOPS WORKED THEIR WAY AROUND THE BLIND SIDE OF THE HILL, TO OUTFLANK THE ITALIANS...

...WHO BROKE AND FLED TOWARD MOUNT MATAJUR, THE FINAL PEAK.

HALT!

THROUGH THE TREES, ROMMEL COULD SEE TROOPS GATHERED—LOTS OF THEM.

THOUSANDS...

...THROWN UP HERE FOR A LAST STAND, AND WE, BUT A FEW HUNDRED, AGAINST THEM.

HE THOUGHT AND ACTED LIKE LIGHTNING.

WAVING A WHITE HANKERCHIEF, HE STRODE AHEAD OF HIS MEN.

IF THEY ATTACK ALL AT ONCE, WE WILL BE CRUSHED. DO THEY NOT REALIZE?

HE QUICKENED TO CLOSE THE GAP BETWEEN THEM.

...MUSTN'T GIVE THEM THE CHANCE TO THINK...

LAY DOWN YOUR ARMS!

SUDDENLY, THE ITALIANS RUSHED TOWARD HIM, HOISTING HIM ABOVE THEIR SHOULDERS.

EVVIVA GERMANIA!*

IN ALL, THE WURTTEMBERGERS CAPTURED 150 OFFICERS AND 9,000 MEN, FOR MINIMAL LOSSES.

YEARS OF USELESS BLOODSHED AND CRUELTY HAD SEEMINGLY ROBBED THE ITALIAN ARMY OF THE WILL TO FIGHT.

THE END

*LONG LIVE GERMANY!

OUTCOMES

During the retreat, Cadorna ordered a last-ditch stand at the Piave River, 20 miles (32 kilometers) from Venice. Ten thousand Italians had been killed, 30,000 wounded, and 265,000 taken prisoner.

The two Austrian commanders, Conrad (left) and Boroevic (right), could not agree on how best to defeat Italy, after the stunning victory at Caporetto.

RE-GROUPING

The two armies settled either side of the Piave. Cadorna was replaced with the capable and humane General Armando Diaz. The British and French came to gauge the state of the Italians and agreed to send weapons and men to the cause.

The Austrian army was carved up between two commanders while the Italian public rallied behind the military. New soldiers joined, replacing the losses. Patriotism surged, led on by a young journalist called Mussolini.

American regiments fought Austrians as part of the general Allied effort to strengthen the Italian Front in 1918.

ATTACK AND COUNTER

Two separate Austrian attacks began on June 15, 1918. Both were brutally repelled by well-organized Italian defenders. Rather than chase the battered Austrians across Piave, Diaz insisted on waiting until his army was prepared enough to deliver a crushing blow. On the anniversary of Caporetto, October 24, the onslaught began. War-weary Austrian troops began refusing to fight. Four days later, the Austro-Hungarian Empire fell, as major regions declared independence. The war in Italy was over.

Unlike Cadorna, Diaz was strategically clever, and also had the confidence of his soldiers.

44

THE MACEDONIAN FRONT

In March 1916, 118,000 Serbs (from an original 1914 starting force of 460,000) arrived at a British-built base at Salonika, in Northern Greece. They joined the British, French, Russian, and Italian divisions. The invasion of Southern Serbia (Macedonia) was to roll forward in 1917.

Meanwhile, there was Greek "neutrality" to deal with. The King favored the Germans, while the Prime Minister (in exile) sided with the Allies. Under British pressure, the King was deposed, and Greece declared war on the Central Powers on June 26, 1917. The offensive got going in September 1918, and despite

A French soldier teaches a Serbian soldier how to use a trench mortar.

Romania (above) entered the war on the Allied side in August 1916, but was forced to surrender just 16 months later, when her close ally, Russia, collapsed in revolution.

offering resistance, the Bulgarians were forced back in retreat. By June 29, Northern Macedonia had been captured. Meanwhile, with their allies either beaten or in chaos, over 4,000 rebellious Bulgarian troops had massed on their capital, Sofia, to overthrow the King. Serbia was officially liberated on November 3, 1918. The British took Constantinople, unopposed, from Ottoman Turkey, which had crumbled under the Arab Revolt.

King Alexander of Serbia enters Macedonia with French General, Sarrail (below). Alexander united the south Slav nations into the first Yugoslavia after the war.

A Greek soldier (left) in ceremonial uniform

GLOSSARY

agony Extreme and or intense pain or suffering

Allies A group of nations fighting against the Central Powers in World War I

artillery High caliber weapons used by military during battle

assassin Someone who murders an important person by a surprise attack

barricade A defense barrier built to stop an enemy

bombardment An attack with concentrated artillery fire or bombs

Central Powers A group of nations fighting in World War I, consisting of the German Empire, Austro-Hungarian Empire, the Ottoman Empire, and the Kingdom of Bulgaria

counterattack An attack made as a reply to another attack

decimation The killing of one out of a group of ten soldiers, chosen for punishment from a unit of an army

evacuation The removal of persons from a dangerous area

exile Prolonged separation from one's country or home, by force or circumstances

expedition A journey or voyage made for some specific purpose, such as war or discovery

feint An attack aimed at one place, merely to create a distraction from the real place of attack

field kitchen A mobile kitchen or food truck used to give military men hot meals

ignite To set on fire, kindle

Australian gunners at Anzac Cove, Gallipoli, in 1915

iron rations Emergency food supplies that cannot be opened without orders

liberated To be released from occupation by a foreign power

massacre The killing of weak or innocent people by those in control

neutrality To refuse to support one side over another in a dispute

offensive A carefully planned military attack

orderly A soldier assigned to perform various chores for a commanding officer

persuaded To be convinced by someone to do something

pitched battle A battle where both sides decide where and when they will fight

rebellious Defying or resisting an established authority

retreat To draw back and pull away

rout A retreat or withdrawl of troops from a battlefield, resulting in a defeat

skulker Someone who is hiding cowardly

smother To cover closely or thickly

spire A structure at the top of a building in the shape of a pyramid

stalemate Any position in which no progress can be made

superior Of higher quality or power

swine A coarse or contemptible person

tragic Dreadful or mournful; pitiful, sad

trench A long, narrow hole dug in the ground to serve as a shelter from enemy fire or attack

vigorous Energetic, active, forceful, powerful

wretched In very unfortunate conditions or circumstances; miserable

French and Italian soldiers on the line of the Piave River, in 1918

INDEX